SANTA IS THE PERSON WHO BRINGS ALL THE GIFT AND JOY TO CHRISTMAS.

SANTA LOVES COOKIES AND MILK

SANTA CLAUSE

RUDOLPH THE REINDEER

SANTA'S SLEIGH

HO HO HO

MERRY

CHRISTMAS

THIS IS A
POPULAR
CHRISTMAS
GREETING

CANDY CANE

JINGLE BELLS

CHRISTMAS TREE

MILK AND COOKIES

THEY ARE SANTA'S LITTLE HELPERS.
THEY HELP SANT BUILD ALL THE
TOYS AND PACKAGE THE PRESENT

CHRISTMAS ELVES

A LIST MADE FOR NAUGHTY
CHILDREN WHO WERE NAUGHTY TO
MOMMY AND DADDYY ALL THE TIME.
THEY DONT GET PRESENTS

NAUGHTY LIST

CHRISTMAS GIFT

ALSO KNOWN

SANTA'S FAVOURITE DOOR

CHIMNEY

A POPULAR CHRISTMAS DECORATION

CHRISTMAS GNOME

SNOWFLAKE

CANDY

TOY TRAIN

CHRISTMAS CAKE

GINGER BREAD HOUSE

CHRISTMAS BOW

SNOWFGLOBE

STAR

CHRISTMAS SOCKS

MR. SNOWMAN

CHRISTMAS IS A TIME TO BE WARM AND COZY WITH FAMILY AND FRIENDS

FIREPLACE

CHRISTMAS CAROL

CHRISTMAS IS THE CELEBRATION OF
BABY JESUS COMING TO THE WORLD

BABY JESUS

SANTA'S
HAT

SANTA'S
BEARDS

ELVE'S HAT

SANTA'S
BELT

IT IS USED TO MAKE THE CHRISTMAS TREE SHINING AND BRIGHT

CHRISTMAS LIGHTS

CHRISTMAS CARD

CANDLES

ANGEL

WREATH

GLOVES

THREE WISE MEN

CHRISTMAS ORNAMENT

A FAVOURITE CHRISTMAS DRINK
THAT IS MADE FROM EGG

EGGNOG

GRINCH

A GRINCH IS SOMEONE
WHO HATES
CHRISTMAS

HOT CHOCOLATE

ICE SKATING

TOYS

PEPPERMINT

MRS. CLAUSE

FELIZ NAVIDAD

SPANISH VERSION OF "MERRY CHRISTMAS"

MANGER

OVEN MITTEN

SLED

BAKING

HAPPY HOLIDAYS

www.ingramcontent.com/pod-product-compliance
Lightning Source LLC
LaVergne TN
LVHW071224160826
845679LV00003B/895

9798370994203